THE PERFECT MARTINI BOOK

THE PERFECT MARTINI BOOK

Robert Herzbrun

Design by Stephanie Tevonian

An Original Harvest/HBJ Book

HARCOURT BRACE

JOVANOVICH

New York and London

The author wishes to thank the following publishers for permission to quote from the sources listed:

Harper & Row: Only Yesterday, *Frederick Lewis Allen*

Little, Brown and Company: Verses from 1929 On, *Ogden Nash,* *© 1935 by Ogden Nash*

Macmillan Publishing Company: Casino Royale, *Ian Fleming,* *© 1953, 1954 by Glidrose Publications Ltd.*

Charles Scribner's Sons: A Farewell to Arms, *Ernest Hemingway*

Cover photograph courtesy of Seagram's Extra Dry Gin

Printed in the United States of America

Library of Congress Cataloging in Publication Data
Herzbrun, Bob.
The perfect martini book.
(An Original Harvest/HBJ book)
1. Martinis. I. Title.
TX 951.H55   641.8'74   79-1858
ISBN 0-15-644642-1

First Original Harvest/HBJ edition
A B C D E F G H I J

CONTENTS

THE PERFECT MARTINI BOOK

INTRODUCTION

 T ALL STARTED with a
sip of wine.
Some unknown ancient
sampling fermented fruit
juice . . . delighted with his
find. When? We don't know.
Wine is as old as the recorded history of man.
The Old Testament tells us that one of Noah's
first chores, after leaving the ark, was
planting his vineyard. And archaeologists
confirm that wine was enjoyed more than ten
thousand years ago, during the Stone Age.

Addison
1 oz. dry gin
1½ oz. sweet
    vermouth
Orange peel

The art of brewing is a bit newer, but it,
too, reaches back to ancient times. Translated
hieroglyphics show the Egyptians not only
made beer but used barley for their malt. And
they were not alone. Ancient manuscripts
reveal brews native to Russia, China, Japan,
and Africa.

Distilling was first mentioned in the
writings of Aristotle around 350 B.C. But the
process is much older than that. In fact, the
Greeks probably learned the art of distilling
from the alchemists of Alexandria, Egypt,
who are thought to have been the first to
fashion a still in their search for a device that

3

would help transform base metals into gold. It was not until the tenth century A.D., however, that the distilling process was applied to alcoholic beverages. But once it was discovered that the alcoholic content of fermented beverages could be multiplied three or four times by distillation, the process spread rapidly. By the twelfth century distilled spirits were common throughout Europe and known as far as China.

Fermenting, brewing, distilling — all date back to the early age of modern man. The cocktail, or mixed drink, is something else again. It's a comparatively recent creation, dating back to the late 1600s, when rum was the favorite drink of English sailors who patrolled the waters of the Caribbean and the Gulf of Mexico. Shipboard supplies were limited, however, and the rum had to be rationed. To stretch the supply, the British started mixing rum with local liquors. These mixtures took the name of *cocktails,* so legend goes, because in Campeche, on Mexico's Yucatán Peninsula, they were stirred with the stem of a plant named *cola de gallo* — the "cock's tail."

Today, *cocktail* represents a great deal more than it did in Campeche. It refers to a time of day. A time when adults seek escape from pressures and daily routine. A time for

4

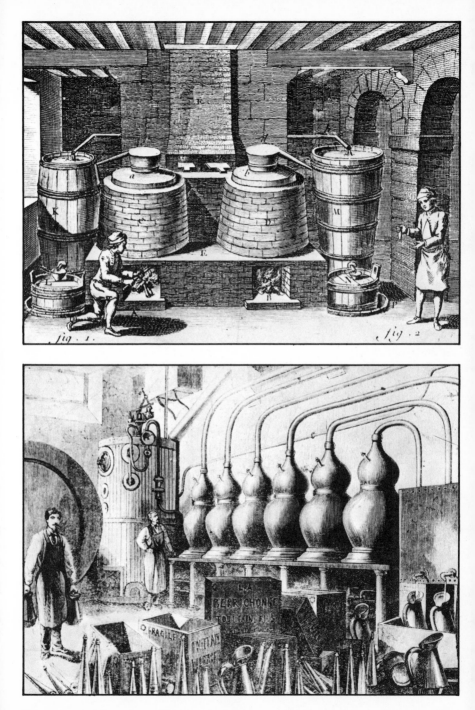

fig. 1.

fig. 2.

5

fellowship. A time for examining the deepest
problems of mankind. A time for small talk.

To millions, the term *cocktail* also refers to
a particular drink that has become "one of a
kind." To them, a cocktail is a Dry Martini
and only a Dry Martini. And the cocktail hour

6

is the Martini Hour. Their reverence toward
the Martini borders on the fanatical. When
they drink, the Martini is all they drink. Yet
most will openly agree that although the
Martini is a very good drink, it should be
even better. The Martini is a phenomenon,
for while it has become the classic cocktail, it
is in constant dispute. From the moment gin
and vermouth were first blended more than a
hundred years ago, the search began . . . the
search for a better Martini: *The Perfect
Martini.*

Ainsworth
1¾ oz. dry gin
¾ oz. dry vermouth

THE BEGINNING

I T WAS ONE of those rare days when the sun rose hot over the Bay and the moist Pacific air was quickly melted away. San Francisco in the mid-1800s was the most exciting of cities, and one of San Francisco's major attractions was its scores of saloons and taverns. The most famous of all was tended by Professor Jerry Thomas.

The professor was a most inventive bartender, hardly the type satisfied with a life behind the bar pouring straight shots for indiscriminate guzzlers. He became noted for his mixtures and blends, and particularly for his specialty, which brought a glowing warmth to many a chilled San Franciscan, a drink he modestly named for himself — the Tom and Jerry.

But this was quite a different kind of day in San Francisco, a blazing hot day — hardly Tom and Jerry weather. And when a tired, wilted stranger entered Jerry Thomas's bar, he asked the world's greatest bartender to mix

Alaska
7 parts dry gin
1 part yellow
 Chartreuse
Twist of lemon peel

9

something that would revive him for the
journey that lay ahead.

San Francisco in 1853.

Thomas thought for a moment, then
reached for a bottle of gin, then a bottle of
vermouth. And he mixed the two with bitters,
Maraschino, and ice.

After the stranger departed, Thomas tasted
the mixture. "Perhaps," he thought, "perhaps it has possibilities." It must have a
name. But what name?

Maybe if Thomas had not already created
the drink that bears his name, the blending of
gin and vermouth might well be called — can
you believe? — a Tom and Jerry. ("Bartender, a very dry and very cold Tom and

10

(Top) "The Club in Session"; a typical nineteenth-century California saloon.

(Bottom) San Francisco's Market Street, 1878.

11

(Top) Gold miners at the bar.

(Bottom) Daguerreotype of miner in full regalia, circa 1860.

Jerry, please . . . with an olive.")

The answer: name it for the stranger. But no one knew the stranger's name, only his destination. And so it was, in the mid-1800s in San Francisco, that gin and vermouth were first mixed and named the Martinez, after a small town some forty miles across the Bay.

As the popularity of the drink moved east, the name Martinez evolved into Martini. And that is how the classic cocktail got its name.

Or is it?

"Not so," insist the citizens of Martinez, who point out that during the gold rush their town was the first of any size between the goldfields and San Francisco. So the saloons of Martinez catered to many a celebrating miner who had struck it rich. The Martinez legend has it that one night a celebrating

Alfonso Special
1 oz. dry gin
1 oz. dry vermouth
½ oz. Grand Marnier
¼ oz. sweet vermouth
1 dash bitters

second annual
MARTINEZ AREA CHAMBER of COMMERCE
MARTINI FESTIVAL
Saturday, May 22, 1976 - 2 - 5 p.m.
CARPENTER'S HALL
3780 Alhambra Avenue, Martinez, California
"Birthplace of the Martini"

Featuring
THE PERFECT
MARTINI
MAKER CONTEST

ALSO
Best Dressed Bartender
and Waitress
Most Graceful Waitress

Pre-Festival Press Party
WEDNESDAY, May 12, 1976 — 4:30 - 7:00 P.M.
BIRDSONG'S LANDING, MARTINEZ MARINA
R.S.V.P. (415) 228-2345

YOU
ARE CORDIALLY INVITED
TO ATTEND –

Pre-Festival Press Party
WEDNESDAY, May 12, 1976 — 4:30 - 7:00 P.M.
BIRDSONG'S LANDING, MARTINEZ MARINA
R.S.V.P. (415) 228-2345

miner ordered Champagne for everyone in
the house. But there was none. So the bartender bragged he had something much better
— a "Martinez Special"— and quickly
mixed a drink using some Sauterne and gin
he had behind the bar. "Great," thought the
miner, who traveled on to San Francisco,
where he continued celebrating, ordering a
"Martinez Special" wherever he went.

Truth or legend, the city holds an annual
Martini Festival to celebrate its heritage as
the "Birthplace of the Martini."

14

The British have another version, claiming the Martini as their creation. They say the drink was named the Martini from the first sip or, as they tell it, the first kick. According to English lore, the drink was named after the famed rifle of the British Imperial Army: the Martini and Henry. The rifle was noted for two things — its accuracy and its kick.

From Italy, another version: According to the classic vermouth makers Martini and Rossi, the drink was so named because it was first made with Martini and Rossi vermouth ... and plenty of it, too. And to back their claim, Martini and Rossi has no less authority than Noah Webster's *New World Dictionary*. What's more, if you look it up in your *Funk and Wagnalls*, they, too, concur. ("Martini ... a cocktail made of dry gin and vermouth ... after Martini and Rossi, a company making vermouth.")

All-American Martini

7 parts Peoria dry gin
1 part Modesto dry vermouth

Garnish with a California green olive or a twist of Sunkist lemon peel. Serve in a plastic cocktail glass.

The controversy as to whether the Martini was named for a town, a rifle, or a vintner will never be settled. No matter. For it has long since been dwarfed by another controversy, one that has enveloped the drink from the moment it was first mixed, poured, and sipped: "How should a Martini be made?"

We can be certain that as the stranger crossed the Bay and rode over the hill on his way to Martinez, he was thinking, "There's a drink that could be pretty good, if only he'd màde it drier."

Just consider, for a moment, that first Martini . . . and imagine what went into it. Professor Thomas was good enough to put his secrets into writing and in 1862 published the first of many editions of his famous work simply titled:

How To Mix Drinks
or
The Bon Vivant's Companion

Containing Clear and Reliable Directions for Mixing all the Beverages Used in the United States, Together with the Most Popular British, French, German, Italian, Russian and Spanish Recipies [*sic*], Embracing Punches, Juleps, Cobblers, etc., etc., etc., etc., in Endless Variety

---

Recipe "Number 105" in this first recipe book of mixed drinks is for the "Martinez Cocktail":

Use small bar glass
One dash of bitters
Two dashes of Maraschino
One wineglass of vermouth
Two small lumps of ice
One pony of Old Tom gin

SHAKE up thoroughly, and strain into a large cocktail glass. Put a quarter of a slice of lemon in the glass, and serve. If the guest prefers it very sweet, add two dashes of gum syrup.

A wineglass of vermouth to a pony, or ounce, of gin means that at the start, Professor Thomas poured about a 4-to-1 Martini. But it was four parts of vermouth to one part gin. What's more, the vermouth was not the dry French vermouth used in Martinis today, but Italian vermouth, the sweet, reddish vermouth popular in Manhattans and other sweet cocktails.

That's just the start: the gin was also different from today's London dry. At that time, sweeteners were added to London gin, making the product referred to as "Old Tom." But there was still more. For added sweetening, a little Maraschino. And so it wouldn't

Allies
2 parts dry gin
1 part French vermouth
2 dashes kümmel
Green olive (plain or stuffed)

get too chilled: "Two small lumps of ice."

With this kind of beginning, how did the Martini survive? Why was man determined to rescue the Martini rather than let it drift into oblivion?

Two reasons.

First, man is gifted with great vision. He foresaw the ultimate creation of the Classic Cocktail.

Second, the name was catchy.

Man was determined. He experimented, he tested, he tasted. And his search led him to a new gin and a new vermouth, both of which helped bridge the gap to a new and different kind of Martini — the Dry Martini.

THE BASICS

 O APPRECIATE the evolution of the Martini, it is necessary to know a good deal more about its very basic ingredients: gin and vermouth.

Gin

Gin is nothing more than diluted alcohol flavored with extracts from different plants. The strongest of these flavorings is the juniper berry, where the name *gin* comes from.

The Dutch, who were the first to make gin in the late 1500s, named it *genièvre*—French for *juniper*. As *genièvre* became popular in England, the name was simplified until it was just plain *gin*.

Through the years there have been two basic types of gin—Dutch and London. They differ in the way they are made and the way they taste. London gin is made in two steps. First, a fermented mash of grain (usually corn), a little rye, and some malt are distilled into virtually tasteless alcohol. This alcohol is mixed with flavoring agents and distilled a second time. The result is gin, very strong gin. So distilled water is added to bring the

Ambassador
7 parts dry gin
1 part French vermouth
1 tsp. dry white wine
Twist of lemon peel

Mix without the wine and pour into a cocktail glass. Gently float the wine from a teaspoon on the surface of the Martini.

19

gin to "bottle proof," and then it's ready for sale.

The Dutch take a more direct approach to making gin. They throw everything together from the beginning — the fermenting grain and all the flavoring agents — and distill it at a much lower proof than the British. The result is a gin close to "bottle proof" right out of the still. And because little dilution is needed, Dutch, or "Hollands," gin is more full-bodied than London dry and has a pronounced malty flavor.

Naturally, each distiller has his own secret formula for the flavoring that gives each brand of gin its distinctive taste. These formulas sound far more like the start of a witch's brew than a Dry Martini. While the amounts differ, the makings might include juniper berries, coriander seeds, orris, orange peel, cassia bark, lemon peel, cardamom capsules, angelica, and caraway seeds.

(In addition to London and Dutch gin, a product named sloe gin can be found in better liquor stores. Despite its name, sloe gin is not a gin at all, but a liqueur made of sloe berries. Originally the berries were blended with gin, but today neutral alcohol is used.)

Because the double distilling of London gin produces a much subtler product, it is by far the more popular gin and the one best

Pl. 396.

Genévrier commun.   Juniperus communis L.

Coriandrum sativum L.

22

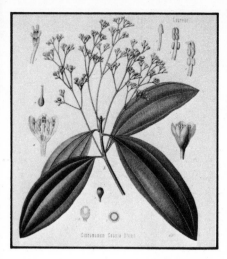 

suited for use in cocktails. At the time the first Martinis were being mixed, however, London gin was quite a different product from what it is today.

Gin came into great popularity in Britain largely as a result of William of Orange, a Dutchman, becoming King of England in 1688 when his predecessor, James II, was tossed out and fled to France. Until that time much of the wine and spirits enjoyed in England had been imported from France, but when France became the enemy, William decreed the end of French trade. To compensate for the loss of French wines and spirits, every Englishman was given the right to distill spirits from home-grown grain — and the floodgates of gin were thrown open. It is estimated that gin consumption in England rose from half a million gallons in 1690 to eight-

(Far left) Coriander.
(Above left) Cassia bark.
(Above right) Cardamom.

Amber Dream
2 parts dry gin
1 part Italian vermouth
1 dash orange bitters
3 dashes yellow
  Chartreuse
Shake.

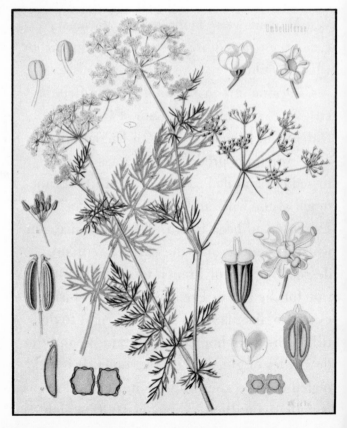

William of Orange, 1650-1702, was instrumental in the development of native English liquors.

een million gallons by 1710—the equivalent of nearly three gallons for every man, woman, and child in the country. Public drunkenness became such a problem that in 1736 the Gin Act was passed limiting production and sales while imposing tremendous taxes on the trickle of gin that was legal. But England's effort to control alcohol consumption in 1736 was no more successful than America's similar experiment with Prohibition nearly two hundred years later. Gin was simple to make, illegally or otherwise, and gin marched on as "the people's spirit." In 1742 consumption of gin in England was even greater than when the gin control law had been passed. And the

Army Cocktail
2 oz. dry gin
½ oz. sweet vermouth
Orange peel

25

Hogarth's famous engraving Gin Lane.

futility of attempting to legislate gin consumption was acknowledged with repeal of the Gin Act, just six years after passage.

During this period gin was usually drunk straight, without ice; so to make it acceptable to the eighteenth-century English palate, it was sweetened with sugar. Sweet gin was the

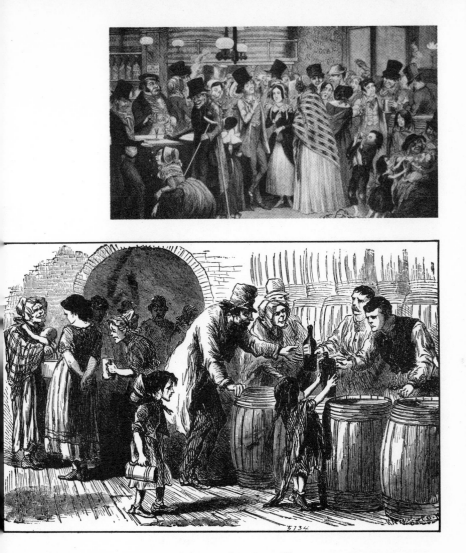

only London gin in those days and it is still sold today under the name Old Tom. It was this sweetened Old Tom gin that was used in that first Martini.

The process used in making this London gin was important, for it allowed for many changes, changes demanded by Martini

(Top and bottom) Scenes of London's gin shops.

drinkers in search of a cocktail that was drier, drier, drier. First, in the mid-1800s, the sugar was eliminated and dry gin was born. Second, the blend of aromatics used to flavor gin has been adjusted through the years to satisfy changing tastes. And finally, the alcoholic content of the gin has been gradually increased as less and less water is used to dilute the potent gin distillate.

In the words of the poet laureate of Martinidom, Ogden Nash:

Vermouth

There is something about a Martini,
A tingle remarkably pleasant;
A yellow, a mellow Martini;
I wish that I had one at present.
There is something about a Martini,
Ere the dining and dancing begin,
And to tell you the truth,
It is not the vermouth—
I think that perhaps it's the gin.
"A Drink with Something in It"

Vermouth takes a terrible beating in the lore and legend of the Martini. But the fact is that vermouth gives a Dry Martini more flavor and character than does gin. As a result, the careful selection and precise measurement of the vermouth has always been one of the keys in the search for the Perfect Martini.

And it was most fortunate that while the English were busy experimenting with gin,

Ogden Nash.

there was great activity on the Continent among the makers of fine vermouth.

Until 1812 there was just one type of vermouth, the Italian, or sweet, vermouth. But in that year Noilly Prat introduced a new kind of vermouth, much drier than the traditional Italian; it was introduced in France and thus labeled French vermouth. Distribution was not quite as fast in those days as it is today: the first bottle of Noilly Prat did not arrive in the United States until 1853. And that was still long before dry vermouth was as well known or as well distributed as its sweeter counterpart.

Both Italian and French vermouth are

Artillery
1½ oz. dry gin
¾ oz. sweet vermouth
1 dash Angostura
   bitters
Twist of lemon peel

(Top) Forget-me-not.
(Bottom) Wormwood.

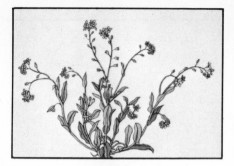

30

made from wine fortified with alcohol and infused with a great number of flavorful herbs, leaves, plants, flowers, roots, seeds, peels, and things that grow in the ground with exotic names like blessed thistle, forget-me-not, wormwood, and starwort. The basic difference between the two vermouths is in the sweetening. Both are made from white wines, but the Italians use sweeter wines and add still more sweetening to the finished product.

If both types of vermouth are made from white wine, why is the Italian vermouth red? The color of both Italian and French vermouth has nothing to do with the taste: it's strictly for eye appeal. Unflavored coloring is added to all vermouth to give it its classic reddish or golden glow.

Astoria
1½ oz. dry gin
¾ oz. dry vermouth
1 dash orange bitters
Green olive

While gin is a simple product to make, vermouth is most difficult. A good dry vermouth is carefully coaxed from nearly fifty ingredients and takes four years from start to finish. It is aged, decanted, filtered, refrigerated, clarified, and pasteurized.

And for what? For a Martini it is almost left out of.

THE MARTINI GOES DRY

ROM THE MOMENT London dry gin, the new unsweetened gin, was introduced, it began to drive Old Tom from the shelves. Today, out of the hundreds of gins that might line the shelves of liquor stores, you might find one Old Tom (probably Boord's Old Tom Gin, which now dominates the minuscule Old Tom market). San Francisco's tony Pacific-Union Club and Clift Hotel still honor Old Tom, featuring Pacific-Union Martinis — Dry Martinis in every way except for the gin, which is Old Tom. Elsewhere, Martini gin is London dry gin.

For even more dryness, man reached for the new vermouth from France and, at first, mixed it half and half with Italian vermouth. The result was the Queen Martini, a vast improvement over the original and one that, to this day, is included in better recipe books:

Atta Boy
2 oz. dry gin
½ oz. dry vermouth
2 dashes grenadine

The Queen Martini
1 part Italian vermouth
1 part French vermouth

2 parts dry gin
1 dash orange bitters
1 dash Angostura bitters

Knickerbocker Hotel,
42nd and Broadway.

Then came the bold stroke. By legend, the momentous event occurred at the posh Knickerbocker Hotel in New York City. The year? Maybe 1900. Maybe 1901. Perhaps the first innovation of the twentieth century. The event: a bartender named Martini di Arma Tiggia (what else?) mixed a Martini using *only* dry gin and *only* dry vermouth. By today's standards it was not a Dry Martini. (But compare it with that first San Francisco Martini.)

The Original Dry Martini
1 part French vermouth
1 part London dry gin
1 dash orange bitters

This was the state of the art at the turn of the century, a Dry Martini made with equal parts dry gin and dry vermouth. And it was not long thereafter that a few bartenders, noticing their customers' preference for an even drier Martini, started pouring the gin with a slightly heavier hand. From there it was just a short time until the classic Dry Martini became the standard, and when a Martini was ordered it was mixed with two parts gin to one part vermouth.

The Classic Dry Martini
1 part French vermouth
2 parts London dry gin
1 dash orange bitters

Even though the Martini had evolved into a rather palatable cocktail by the turn of the century, its popularity was not yet widespread. Martinis were sipped at the elegant new Waldorf-Astoria Hotel in New York and the kingly Palace Hotel in San Francisco, but in the heart of America men drank whiskey.

So the Martini moved on to Europe, where gin and vermouth are native. By the early 1900s it became popular in the carefree bars of Paris and London, where it was known as Gin and French or Gin 'n' It. And as the War to End Wars ripped the Continent, thousands of Americans sailed for Europe, whereupon the bars of Paris and London were suddenly filled with Yanks. The bars had no Bourbon or rye. So the soldiers experimented with mixed drinks and discovered "Le Martini." Hemingway's Frederick Henry says it all: "I· ... [drank] a couple more martinis. I had never tasted anything so cool and lean. They made me feel civilized."

No wonder, when the war was over and the Yanks returned home, that they introduced "Le Martini" wherever they went. But a

powerful movement was sweeping America. For over a hundred years there had been organized agitation to outlaw the consumption of alcoholic beverages in the United States. Until World War I, attempts on a nationwide scale had failed. The war became a rallying point for the prohibitionists' cause, however, as they managed to position alcohol, along with the Germans, as the enemy of America, with reasoning such as: "Alcohol prevents the American soldier from performing at his peak," "Beer is German, thus evil," and "Grain used to make alcohol would be better used to make bread for the starving children of the Allies." The result: thirty-six

Atty
2 oz. dry gin
½ oz. dry vermouth
2 dashes crème de
violette
Twist of lemon peel

states ratified the Eighteenth Amendment to the Constitution and on January 16, 1920, the law of the United States dictated, "No more drinking." Bars and taverns from coast to coast closed their doors. Ironically, it was this

Restaurant padlocked due to violation of National Prohibition Act.

38

law prohibiting the consumption of alcoholic
beverages that turned millions from whiskey
to the cocktail — and made the Dry Martini
the king of the cocktail.

All liquor being produced was being produced illegally. And since it was far easier to
make passable gin than passable whiskey, gin
became the chief product of the cellar stills
and bathtub blends. But though much of the
illegal liquor was drinkable, it was not good,
and there was a switch to mixed cocktails that
contained other ingredients that masked the
harsh taste of the second-rate liquor. In addition, a great social change occurred during
Prohibition: women started drinking. Frederick Lewis Allen vividly reflects on the times
in his history of the twenties, *Only Yesterday:*

*Angry placard carriers
in an anti-Prohibition
parade.*

Bacardi Dry
2 oz. Bacardi rum
 (light)
½ oz. dry vermouth

"Among well-to-do people the serving of cocktails before dinner became almost socially obligatory. Mixed parties swarmed up to the curtained frills of speakeasies and uttered the mystic password, and girls along with men stood at the speakeasy bar with one foot on the brass rail. The late afternoon cocktail party became an American institution."

Cocktail sipping was by no means limited to the ladies of the well-to-do. In the words of Elmer Davis: "The days when father spent his evenings at Cassidy's bar with the rest of the boys are gone, and probably forever; Cassidy may still be in business at the old stand and father may still go down there on evenings, but since prohibition mother goes down with him."

Prohibition was also responsible for the "Who-can-mix-the-best-Martini" syndrome. For the first time, cocktails were being mixed

(Far left, top) Prohibition agent seizing illicit still in Brooklyn.
(Far left, bottom) Part of a huge haul seized in Savannah, Georgia.
(Above) One of Washington, D.C.'s, largest stills.

Bacardi Sweet
2 oz. Bacardi rum (light)
½ oz. sweet vermouth

41

(Far left) "Joe sent me."

(Left) Interior of an authentic twenties speakeasy.

(Bottom) Federal agents smashing twenties speakeasy.

in the privacy of the home, and everyone began looking for a unique Martini he could call his own. Martinis were being made not only with vermouth but with sherry and dry white wines. Pieces of fruit began to appear in glasses — green olives, red cherries, lemon twists, orange peels, pearl onions.

The master of the house sought the reputa-

(Left) Women's first entry into New York's saloons, pre-Prohibition days.

(Bottom) Women at the bar; a commonplace scene at a speakeasy.

(Far right) Celebrating repeal of Prohibition, New York City.

tion as master of the Martini. He mixed them drier and drier and drier. Some went so far as to mix Martinis with three parts of gin to one part vermouth.

How dry could a Martini get?

It did not take long to find out. On December 5, 1933, Prohibition was repealed, cellar stills were closed, and bathtubs were used for bathing again. Legitimate bars once again opened their doors, staffed by expert bartenders who looked upon the mixing of a cocktail as an art.

The cocktail hour, born during Prohibition, came up from underground. And special meeting places became as celebrated for their

Bald Head
4 parts dry gin
1 part French
   vermouth
1 part Italian vermouth
1 or 2 dashes Pernod
Green olive
Sprinkle the oil from a
twist of lemon peel
on top.

(Left) Buying liquor, legally.

(Bottom) Drinking aboard the S.S. Manhattan after thirteen years' abstinence.

(Far right) Citizens of East St. Louis, Illinois, usher in the repeal.

cocktails as for their culinary specialties. The Martini was the favorite cocktail—a favorite, for instance, of the literary greats who gathered at the famed Round Table of the Algonquin Hotel in New York to sip and lunch and exchange barbs and wit. It was a particular favorite of Alexander Woollcott's; pulling off his soaked coat one rainy day, he was quoted as saying, "I must get out of these wet clothes and into a Dry Martini."

The speakeasy-gone-legit and instant hotel bars were the first to capitalize on repeal, but as the thirties progressed, the trend to turn drinking places into showplaces began. Club-like men's bars were joined by tony cocktail

Ballantine's Cocktail
1½ oz. dry gin
¾ oz. French vermouth
1 dash orange bitters
1 dash Pernod

lounges. Then the "gimmick bar" became popular. The cocktail lounge at the Edgewater Beach Hotel in Chicago was "boarded" by a gangway and created the illusion of being on board a ship. Boston's Copley Plaza and San Francisco's Fairmont were among the hotels featuring merry-go-round bars. The tin roof of a Beverly Hills cocktail lounge was pelted by monsoon-driven rains every hour on the hour. And rooftop bars became the rage — the most famous, San Francisco's Top of the Mark with its unmatchable view of city, Bay, and the Golden Gate.

Music was also a key feature at cocktail lounges in the thirties. Wherever cocktails were served, there was also a piano player — at an upright, grand, or the ubiquitous piano bar. Or a group. Or a dance band. Or a complete floor show.

Gimmick drinks were introduced, too. In

1938 Vic Bergeron transformed his modest Hinky Dink's Tavern in Oakland into Trader Vic's and he and Don the Beachcomber in Chicago introduced America to the likes of Mai Tais, Scorpions, Fog Cutters, and Dr. Fongs.

Still, the Martini stayed number one, America's premier cocktail.

By the late thirties, however, the name *Dry Martini* no longer referred to the two-to-one or three-to-one blend so popular at the start of the decade. The continuing search for the Perfect Martini demanded a drier cocktail, and the Very Dry Martini became the accepted recipe for what had by now become the classic cocktail.

The Very Dry Martini
5 parts dry gin
1 part French vermouth
Twist of lemon peel

Thoroughly chill a stemmed glass in a bed of shaved ice. Mix five parts dry gin with one part French vermouth in a pitcher half filled with ice cubes. Stir vigorously until cold. Pour into the chilled glass. Twist the lemon peel so one or two drops of lemon oil fall to the surface. Drop the peel in the drink.

Baron
1½ oz. dry gin
½ oz. French
    vermouth
¼ oz. orange curaçao
¼ oz. sweet vermouth
Twist of lemon peel

Martinis were not only mixed in different ways, but they began to get fancy names. Several variations of the Martini were no longer called a Martini, the best known of

these being the Gibson — somewhat drier
than the Very Dry Martini, with a small
pickled cocktail onion plopped in the glass.

The Gibson
7 parts dry gin
1 part French vermouth
Cocktail onion

THE MARTINI COMES OF AGE

ORLD WAR II was over, and suddenly the Martini was not just the sophisticate's drink, but everybody's drink. Bankers, plumbers, artists, engineers, chemists, secret agents — everyone drank Martinis.

Suddenly, more London gin was being made in Peoria, Illinois, than in London, England. And French vermouth flowed from towns like Modesto in the heart of California wine country. (Would you like an All-American Martini? Seven parts Peoria dry gin; one part Modesto dry vermouth. Serve in a plastic glass.)

Suddenly, the Martini was everywhere.

The cause of this eruption of Martini-itis was a direct outgrowth of World War II. For while thousands were exposed to "Le Martini" during the First World War, the number rose to millions in the 1940s, and the result was a mass change in American drinking habits.

Barry
1½ oz. dry gin
¾ oz. sweet vermouth
1 dash Angostura
  bitters
White crème de menthe

Stir into a glass. Float crème de menthe on top. Garnish with a twist of lemon peel.

51

"*Wilfred, what did I tell you about letting me drink!*"

Nowhere was this change more dramatically pointed up than in the literature of the post-war period. Being macho once meant drinking straight whiskey. Now the world's most attractive man drank a very special kind of Martini.

James Bond in *Casino Royale* revealed his spiritual secret:

"A dry martini," he said. "One. In a deep Champagne goblet."

"Oui, monsieur."

"Just a moment. Three measures of Gordon's, one of vodka, half a measure of Kina Lillet.

Stars George Brent and Virginia Scott toast at the bar.

Shake it very well until it's ice-cold, then add a large thin slice of lemon-peel. Got it?"

"Certainly, monsieur." The barman seemed pleased with the idea.

"Gosh, that's certainly a drink," said Leiter.

Bond laughed. "When I'm . . . er . . . concentrating," he explained, "I never have more than one drink before dinner. But I do like that one to be large and very strong and very cold and very well made. I hate small portions of anything, particularly when they taste bad. This drink's my own invention. I'm going to patent it when I can think of a good name."

He watched carefully as the deep glass became frosted with the pale golden drink, slightly aerated by the bruising of the shaker. He reached for it and took a long sip.

"Excellent," he said to the barman, "but if you can get vodka made with grain instead of potatoes, you will find it still better."

Bich's Special
1½ oz. dry gin
¾ oz. Lillet
1 dash Angostura
  bitters
Orange peel

James Bond originated his creation combining gin, vodka, and Lillet vermouth, but he did not invent the shaken Martini. The shaken Martini has been around a long time, and there

53

is a small but fanatic cult who, like Bond, insist on having their Martinis shaken. The idea that shaking a Martini "bruises" the gin is, of course, nonsense. It doesn't even bruise the vermouth. What shaking does is get the Martini colder, faster. And it blends the ingredients better.

Unfortunately, a shaken Martini appears cloudy without that crisp, clear, appetizing look of the stirred Martini. That, however, is its only disadvantage. The taste is very much there.

The Advent of Vodka

Bond was not the first to use vodka in a Martini, either. Vodka's popularity can be traced to the Martini-for-lunch bunch, who delighted in the fact they could have a "nooner" without dragging gin breath back to the office. Just as the art of making gin is in the flavoring, the art of making vodka is in eliminating the flavoring. And no flavor, no telltale breath.

Until a few years ago, Americans hardly knew what vodka was. Only three facts were generally known: (1) the Russians invented it; (2) the Russians made it from potatoes; and (3) the Russians made it very strong.

All wrong.

The birthplace of vodka is unclear; both

ONE-MARTINI LUNCH

Bill Lyken's Delight

1½ oz. dry gin
½ oz. dry vermouth
¼ oz. sweet vermouth
Twist of lemon peel
Orange peel

Poland and Russia have strong claims. And potatoes, long fabled as the source of vodka, are actually seldom used. Vodka is simple to make; the distiller merely picks the most plentiful and cheapest ingredient available to him, generally some form of grain. In Russia, it's rye.

In the United States, vodka is usually made from corn or wheat, distilled to a very high-proof alcohol, then passed over charcoal until any residual flavor is gone. Then it's diluted to the desired proof and bottled.

Russian vodka is no stronger than American

vodka, neither in taste nor in proof. Vodka, having little or no flavoring, is virtually taste-less. As for alcoholic strength, most vodka, including that enjoyed in Russia, is bottled at 80 proof. And that's less than most whis-key, less than most gin. Vodka's reputation for strength probably comes from the way Russians drink it. Ice cold. Straight. And in a single swallow. (Come to think of it, if they just added a drop of vermouth, they'd have a . . . but no, they'd want it drier.)

Martinis at Lunch

The lunchtime Martini, whether vodka or gin, has influenced a great deal more than the size of the lunch tab. One can only speculate on its influence in business, politics, and society. For the Martini affects people in different and often interesting ways. Some become giddy. Others belligerent. Some all-knowing. Others sleepy. Some philosophical. Others generous.

The great lunchtime Martini must be a cold Martini. But to prepare a Martini prop-erly, and to get it as cold as it should be, takes a moment. And that's more time than the modern-day bartender has, even when there's no one else at the bar.

The solution to this problem: "on the rocks." Martinis poured into Old-Fashioned glasses packed with cracked ice. The "rocks" not only make it cold but keep it cold and the Martini drinkers have another choice: Martinis "on the rocks" or "straight up."

The Multi-faceted Martini

New and unique ways were discovered to garnish the Martini, and today you never know what you're going to find in your glass — tiny pickled tomatoes called "tom olives"; marinated mushrooms; olives stuffed with almonds, pimientos, anchovies, or Roquefort cheese; pickled beans; miniature ears of corn . . . any and all can be found in today's Martini.

Yet the modern Martini doesn't stop there. Once the barrier was down and vodka was substituted for gin, it was a short step to the Tequila Martini, the Aquavit Martini, and the Rum Martini. Many like the gin, but don't care for the vermouth; hence the Sake Martini, the Chartreuse Martini, even the Scotch Martini.

Blenton
1½ oz. dry gin
¾ oz. dry vermouth
1 dash Angostura
   bitters
Twist of lemon peel

The purist is aghast. All he wants is the driest Martini man can conceive. But how can he make it drier? Perhaps pass the cap from a bottle of vermouth over chilled gin? Not dry enough. Perhaps ice the gin in the shadow of a bottle of vermouth? Not dry enough.

Finally, there was even something for the purist: gin distilled and delicately flavored with aromatics with but one purpose in mind:

A "cellarette" carrying nearly a hundred pieces of equipment for the mixing and serving of drinks.

to be poured as a Naked Martini. No vermouth, no bitters. Nothing but gin . . . pure dry gin.

Is the Naked Martini the answer to the search for true dryness? After a hundred years, has the search ended? Has the Perfect Martini been found? If only two Martini drinkers remained on earth, there would still be two "best ways" to mix a Martini.

Perhaps Bernard de Voto put it best. "The proper union of gin and vermouth," he wrote, "is a great and sudden glory; it is one of the happiest marriages on earth and one of the shortest lived."

Unfortunately, it is difficult to find that "great and sudden glory" in commercial establishments where the Martini is most commonly called a "Mart" or "Marty." But through the years there have been some unusual ones.

For over thirty years in New York City, Maria Brogalini served a Purple Martini in her Cin Cin restaurant. Maria called it "The Martini of Love."

Bonnie Prince
1½ oz. dry gin
½ oz. Lillet
¼ oz. Drambuie

For bigger appetites, a Minneapolis restaurant served a six-gallon Martini for just $195. There was a catch, however: one to a customer.

And at Chasen's, Hollywood's famous show-business restaurant, the feature is the Orange Martini.

In many bars of the Orient, bartenders remove a bit of gin from a freshly opened bottle and replace it with dry vermouth. They then close the bottle and pack it in ice until the contents are frigid. When a customer orders a Martini, it is poured full strength from the bottle, never diluted by melting ice.

Perhaps the most elegant Martini was a feature at Delmonico's in Mexico City, where specially designed carts were wheeled right to the table by accomplished bartenders. Frosted glasses were produced from the freezer in the base, and the Martini was mixed with your favorite gin and vermouth at tableside.

The Martini of the Future

Fine spirits carefully mixed in generous portions are gradually giving way to the Twenty-first-Century Martini. More and more bartenders now fire drinks from "bar guns" controlled by buttons which, when pressed in various combinations, suck everything from Bourbon to gin up through a hose connected to hidden bulk containers below. To serve an Extra-Dry Martini, all the bartender has to know is which buttons to push.

But that's just the tip of the iceberg. The National Cash Register Company is marketing its bartender of the future: a bar equipped with a console, a mighty NCR machine. When the call rings out, "One Marty, extra dry," the attendant will merely press the proper keys and automation goes to work. The glass moves into place. Ice cubes drop. The precise measure of gin and the precise measure of vermouth are dispensed into the glass. The amount of liquor dispensed is subtracted from

Boomerang

4 parts dry gin
1 part French
  vermouth
1 part Italian vermouth
2 dashes maraschino
  cherry juice
Twist of lemon peel

inventory and added to sales. And, oh yes, out pops your automatically printed check. The Twenty-first-Century Martini. Coming soon to your favorite bar.

With this sort of progress, the search for the Perfect Martini will shift from public premises to private home . . . where a Dry Martini can still be mixed with care and integrity.

MIXING THE PERFECT MARTINI

HEN THE Perfect Martini is finally mixed, it will be with a great deal of care and patience . . . and carefully selected ingredients.

How do you pick from the countless gins and vodkas lined up on the shelf of the corner liquor store? How do you select the proper vermouth?

Gin

The names alone are enough to confound. Gordon's and Gilbey's, Beefeater and Tanqueray, Bombay and Boodles, Old Lady and even Bath Tub — all are brands of gin that might be encountered while browsing among the bottles of your favorite liquor store. Which is the proper one to choose?

Advertising claims to be illuminating: if you're steeped in tradition and like gins with a heritage, you'll find that Beefeater is a "400-year-old English tradition," that Gordon's is "still based on Papa Gordon's

"Gin."

original 1769 formula," and that Fleisch-
mann's is the "world's first dry gin."

On the other hand, if you like a gin tailored
to the Martini, there's Seagram's, "the perfect Martini gin," and Bombay, "for the
straight-on-the-rocks Martini." Or, if you're
particularly discriminating, you might consider Tanqueray. After all, it's for people who
"select gin as they do fine wines." And if you
believe that the taste buds of the English are
better tuned to the subtle nuances of fine gin,
you'd better check out Squire's TRUE English
Gin. After all, "In England Squire's outsells
Beefeater and Tanqueray combined." But

(Bottom) Henry Stephenson pours a serious drink for Ann Harding.

"If you really cared for me, you'd take me some place where they sell gin."

THE GENIAL HOST: *"Well, ol' top, there's the alcohol, citric acid, glycerine, oil of juniper, essence of orange, oil of coriander, distilled water, and an empty gin bottle. Mix it to suit yourself."*

while Squire's outsells Beefeater and Tanqueray in England, Gordon's boasts that it outsells everyone, everywhere: "Gordon's Gin. Largest seller in England, America, the world."

Advertising leaves some questions unanswered. So let's get to hard facts and the differences among various brands of London dry gin.

For starters, you should be aware that all London dry gin is *not* made in London, nor in Manchester or Liverpool, for that matter. In fact, nine out of every ten bottles of London dry gin enjoyed in the United States today are distilled and bottled in the United States.

And today, the dry gin capital of the world is Peoria, Illinois. (But who would buy "Peoria dry gin"?)

Is London-made gin any better than Peoria-made gin?

Actually, gin that's distilled and bottled by reputable companies differs only in two meaningful ways: flavor and proof.

There is a definite difference in flavor between the more expensive gins and the popularly priced domestic gins. Even identical brands made in different countries can taste different. But selecting flavor is a matter of personal taste. If you're a traditionalist and still enjoy the taste of vermouth, chances are you'll like a gin that's light on aromatics. If you pour a Martini with very little vermouth, you might like a gin that has more flavor.

Boston Bullet
2 oz. dry gin
½ oz. dry vermouth
Almond-stuffed
green olive

One excellent way to compare the flavor of gins, London or Peoria, is to pretend you're sampling perfume. Splash a small amount of gin on the back of your hand, shake off the excess, and, after a moment, whiff the aroma. To catch the flavor of the gin, a whiff is as good as a swallow.

Brands of gin also vary by proof. The higher the proof, the more concentrated the gin. The higher the proof, the stronger the taste. (Proof equals one-half percent, so 90-proof gin is 45 percent alcohol.) The proof of every brand is marked on the label. Is a high-proof gin a better gin? That's a question of how you mix your Martini.

But the minute you begin to mix high-proof gin with low-proof vermouth and no-proof ice, you lower the proof of the Martini. If you like your Martini "straight up," the only diluting will be in the mixing, so you might want to start with a lower-proof gin. And if you like your Martini on the rocks, you might go for a higher-proof gin, for it will quickly be tamed by melting ice.

Vodka

In selecting gin, two things count: flavor and proof. When selecting vodka, forget about the flavor. In fact, if the vodka has a pronounced flavor, forget about the vodka. The best vodka has the least flavor.

Because vodka is quite simple to distill, thousands of brands are available and they come from all over the world. What's more, you must read the labels very carefully to know where they're from.

What sounds more Russian, for instance, than Smirnoff, Wolfschmidt, and Relska? But they're all made in the U.S.A.

Maison Cassini suggests a vodka made in a quaint French home nestled in the sunny hills of Italy. But, alas, it's distilled in England, as are other vodkas with British names like

"Well, dear, how is it?"

Borzoi and Masquers. About the only brands that sound true to their native lands are Wódka Wyborowa (from Poland, of course) and Stolichnaya, the Russian import.

What you *can* learn from the label is the alcoholic content of the vodka, which is important because many brands are available in more than one proof. Most American vodka is 80 proof, with some bottled at 100. English vodka is generally 91.5 proof. Polish vodka? It's all produced by the State Spirits Monopoly, and they have one vodka in their line called Polish White Spirit. Keep an eye open for it. When drunk "neat" at 160 proof, it can be a devastating experience.

Bradford
Combine dry gin and dry vermouth in favorite proportions in a cocktail shaker. Shake until frigid and pour.

69

What proof is best for the Martini? Since vodka is virtually tasteless, the proof does not affect the flavor of the Martini . . . only the spirit.

Vermouth

Choosing the proper vermouth, however, is a little more complicated. For while very little vermouth might be used, it gives the Martini more character than the gin or the vodka.

The differences in dry vermouth are strictly in flavor; they are all about the same proof. And when it comes to taste, everyone seems to want the driest vermouth. After all, "dry" is the key to a great Martini. As a result, vermouth can be labeled "extra dry," "double dry," and even "triple dry."

The fact is, dry vermouth is not all that dry. It was, in fact, designated "dry" for the simple reason that it was drier than its forerunner, sweet vermouth. If you wish to mix your gin or vodka with something really dry, choose a fine, dry white wine. But vermouth, more than anything else, does have the characteristic of blending magnificently with gin to make the classic cocktail.

To find the vermouth that suits your taste best, mix different brands with gin, always in the same proportion. And when you settle on the flavor you prefer, stick with that brand even if it's an expensive import. You use so

(Top) Poster for vermouth by Maga, 1925.

(Bottom) "Noilly Prat is a necessary component of a dry martini. Without it you can make a side car, a gimlet, a white lady, or a gin and bitters, but you cannot make a dry martini."
—W. Somerset Maugham
Points of View, 1958

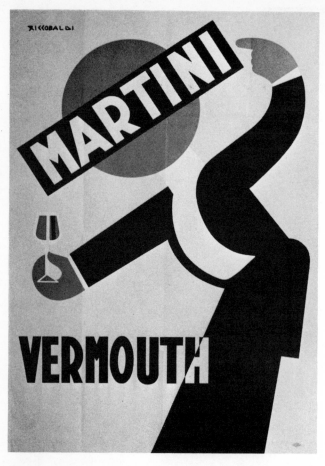

Poster by Riccobaldi for Martini vermouth, circa 1930.

little of it that the added cost is almost incidental.

Once you've selected your brand, it's essential that you care for it. Vermouth is like any wine, relatively stable when sealed in the bottle but still alive and active once opened. There are two things you can do to control subtle changes in the flavor you so carefully picked out.

First, unless you are a big vermouth user,

purchase the smallest size bottle you can find. In many places you can get "miniatures." They are perfect for the just-a-hint-of-vermouth Martini drinker.

Second, once you've opened the bottle of vermouth, store it in the refrigerator. The chilling helps the vermouth hold its original flavor far longer than if it is kept at room temperature.

We've looked at the essentials of a fine Dry Martini: gin or vodka and dry vermouth. Many discriminating Martini-ites will add a third ingredient — a dash of bitters.

Bitters are the mystery ingredient in a Martini. They are called *bitters* because they are, indeed, very bitter. When added to a cocktail, however, they paradoxically create a mellowing effect, smoothing out harshness. While this phenomenon is difficult to understand, it is delightful to taste.

Bitters are made by infusing the flavor of a number of plants into a high-proof alcohol. The formula for each brand of bitters is slightly different, and so is the taste. And because bitters are such a concentrated flavoring, it takes just a drop or two to smooth out a cocktail.

All brands can be classified into two

Bitters

Bronx
1 part dry gin
1 part Italian vermouth
1 part French
  vermouth
¼ orange

Combine the liquid ingredients, squeezing the orange quarter into a cocktail shaker. Drop in the squeezed orange. Shake with cracked ice until chilled. Pour through a strainer into a frosted cocktail glass.

groups: citric and aromatic.

Citric bitters are made for a single purpose — to enhance the flavor of food and
drink. The best known and most used are the
orange bitters.

Aromatic bitters are heavy with quinine,
which gives them not only a distinct flavor,
but medicinal properties as well. The best
known of the aromatic bitters is made by none
other than Angostura-Wupperman, and if you
put a magnifying glass to its label, you'll find
this product is "famous throughout the civilized world . . . as a pleasant and dependable
stomachic."

Just think of it. A dash of Angostura bitters

*(Above and far right)
William Powell and
Myrna Loy as Nick and
Nora Charles of* Thin
Man *fame, cinema's
most celebrated drink-
ing couple.*

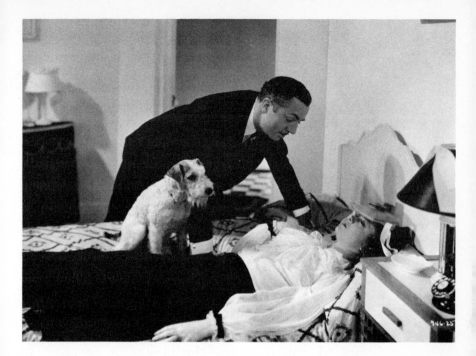

can not only smooth out your Martini but can
also smooth your stomach. What more can
you ask?

The Garnish

Now that we have all the alcoholic ingredients of a fine Martini well in hand, let's
consider the garnish — the dash of color or
taste that makes the Martini complete.

The first Martini mixed over a century ago
had a plump red cherry right in the middle of
it, something seldom seen, or desired, these
days. But the maraschino cherry is about the
only thing you don't see floating in a Martini,
for Dry Martinis are now garnished with a
grand assortment of fruit, falling generally

*(Opposite page) Mae West being questioned on her involvement in a shakedown scheme (*I'm No Angel — 1933 movie with Mae West and Cary Grant):*
Interrogator: "How are you mixed up in all this?"
Mae West: "Like an olive in a Dry Martini."*

into two groups: olive or twist.

Most popular is the green olive stuffed with a bright red pimiento. Green olives are also used plain, or stuffed with almonds, Roquefort cheese, or anchovies. Sometimes you'll find a small pickled tomato in your Martini disguising itself as an olive. It even disguises its name, calling itself a "tom olive." Also round and firm and popular in Martinis, but not olive green, is the pickled cocktail onion.

All of these Martini garnishes have two things in common. First, they are selected not so much for the flavor they impart to the Martini but for their individual taste as an accompaniment to the Martini. Second, their successful use depends only on one's ability to spear them with a toothpick and toss them into a glass.

Adding a twist to a Martini is quite a different story. The twist might be looked upon more as an ingredient than a garnish, for it

markedly changes the flavor of the Martini. Its use also requires a bit of technique.

While orange and lime twists can also be used to flavor Martinis, the most common is the lemon twist. It must be cut carefully from the peel of a fresh lemon so that the narrow strip of peel is separated from the white layer of pulp that lies directly beneath it. This is most important, as the lemon oil is only in the peel.

Once you have poured your chilled Martini, take the lemon peel and pinch it sharply over the glass. A few drops of the lemon oil will sprinkle on the surface. And if you care for a stronger lemon taste, run the peel around the rim of the glass and then drop it right into the Martini.

When considering the garnish, however, remember the thirsty connoisseur who asked for a Very Dry Martini. "Make it with twenty parts gin and one of vermouth," he said.

The bartender carefully measured out the portions, stirred with ice until the mixing glass coated with frost, poured it carefully into a chilled stemmed glass, and asked, "Would you like a twist of lemon peel in that?"

"Look," growled the customer, "if I wanted a lemonade, I'd have asked for a lemonade!"

Glassware

Now that you've selected the perfect ingredients, you must have something to serve them in. Perhaps fine crystal. After all, the perfect Martini must be a masterpiece not only to the taste, but to the eye as well.

A fine Martini should be presented as a fine gift. Always clear, so that the eye can enjoy the frosty transparency of the chilled Martini, accented by a flash of twisted lemon peel or an olive streaked with red pimiento.

The "straight-up" Martini should be served in a long-stemmed glass, for if a Martini is going to be good, it must be cold. And that long, graceful stem will insulate the cold Martini from a warm hand.

A Martini "on the rocks" can be served in a clear Old-Fashioned glass, although there are short-stemmed glasses that are not only more elegant but more practical — they stay

Brown Cocktail
¾ oz. dry gin
¾ oz. light rum
¾ oz. dry vermouth

79

dry at the base and don't leave glass rings on the furniture.

Be sure to pick a large enough cocktail glass. They range from two-and-a-half-ounce "commercial bar" size to four-and-a-half-ounce home size, and even if you never pour a four-and-a-half-ounce Martini, the larger size gives that extra room that keeps a wandering Martini in the glass and off the carpet.

If you're serving Martinis "on the rocks," you'll need a glass that holds just as large a drink but still has extra room for ice cubes. A six-ounce glass is ideal for serving Martinis at home.

Martini Hardware

In addition to glassware, there are a few other bar essentials you will need to enjoy that Perfect Martini in the privacy of your own home.

Most Martinis are "stirred" with ice in a specially designed Martini pitcher. The ideal one is long and lean and made of glass. It has a pouring spout with a stiff pouring lip which catches and holds the ice cubes in the pitcher and out of the Martini. And it's designed so that the mixings can be stirred vigorously without sloshing over the edge. And along with this, you'll need a stirring rod or long-handled mixing spoon that will easily reach

"Thank heaven! I've finally discovered something they like to do."

the bottom of the pitcher. (Oh, the shame of letting a short-handled spoon slip from your fingers and sink to the bottom of a pitcher filled with gin and vermouth and ice!)

James Bond was not alone when he insisted his Martini be shaken, not stirred. So the well-equipped Martini maestro will keep a cocktail shaker handy, as well as a pitcher.

There are two types of cocktail shakers: a heavy glass or stainless metal shaker with a tight-fitting pouring cap; and a two-shaker set, one fitting snugly into the other. Usually one of these shakers is glass, the other stainless steel. With this one you'll also need an always-handy bar strainer with a stainless coil

Cabaret Cocktail
2 oz. dry gin
¼ oz. dry vermouth
¼ oz. Benedictine
2 dashes Angostura
   bitters
Cherry

that clamps over the edge and keeps the ice out of the Martini.

Of the two types, the double shaker is faster to use and more fun. But whichever shaker you use, don't be timid. Use lots of ice and shake vigorously. The idea is to chill the Martini as fast as possible, before the ice begins to melt.

There are a number of other bar accessories you'll need to whip up the Perfect Martini. Two musts: the jigger and the pony. The jigger is one and a half ounces, the pony just one ounce. In addition, a set of measuring spoons is handy.

Besides the measures, you'll want to remember some of the key measurements:

Dash	.17 tsp.
Teaspoon	.125 oz.
Pony	1 oz.
Jigger	1.5 oz.
Pint	16 oz.
Fifth	25.6 oz.
Quart	32 oz.
Liter	33.8 oz.
1.75 liters	59.2 oz.
1/2 gallon	64 oz.

What else will you need?

To carve a twist, you'll need a sharp knife, preferably with a serrated edge. One word of warning: the twists are very thin, and they

Joan Crawford in Our Dancing Daughters.

dry out quickly. Don't peel them in advance; peel them as you use them.

If you're the olive Martini-ite, all you need in addition to the olives are toothpicks. Different colors are a good idea; after a sip or two, guests will still know which Martini is theirs.

Finally, you're going to need a utensil or two to properly ice the Martini. Yes, ice, where most Martinis go wrong.

Even the simplest Martini is made of three ingredients — gin, vermouth, and ice. Great care is spent selecting the gin and vermouth. But the ice is too often made from chlorinated tap water stored in a refrigerator freezer alongside smelly foods whose odors impregnate everything within a three-foot radius. ("Would you care for a Martini eau de Cantaloupe . . . or perhaps a Martini Sardini?")

A great Martini can be made only from ice that is free of bad taste and bad odor. Ideally, the cubes should be made from spring water in an ice tray to avoid that city-water taste; they'll look crystal clear and appetizing. Try not to store that tray next to the cheese, either. If you must, rinse the cubes before using.

When you mix a Martini, you want to get it frigid without getting it watery. The first step is to chill the glasses. If you have a large enough freezer, rinse the bowls of the glasses and set them in the freezer. If your freezer space is limited, bury the glasses in crushed ice.

To do that, of course, you'll need an ice

crusher. You can get an expensive electric one, or a simple little gadget called an ice tapper. The tapper is nothing more than a steel ball on the end of a long, flexible plastic handle. A light tap, and the ice will crack in two. A sharp snap, and the ice will crumble, just right for chilling those glasses.

Now to the Martini. Always use ice right out of the freezer, never ice that has been lying around in a bowl or ice bucket. And use lots of it. The more ice and the colder the ice, the better the Martini. That's because you'll be chilling your Martini with ice, not ice water.

If you're stirring your Martini, use ice cubes in the pitcher. If you're shaking, crack the ice. And try not to mix more than one

Joan Crawford, Wallace Beery, and Lionel Barrymore share drinks at the bar of the Grand Hotel.

Caprice
**1½ oz. dry gin
½ oz. dry vermouth
½ oz. Benedictine
1 dash orange bitters**

"How's your childhood going?"

round at a time. If you do, always pour your "bonus" into an extra container so it isn't diluted by melting ice. Then pack that container in ice to keep it chilled and ready to pour. If that's inconvenient, simply stir it with fresh ice when it's bonus time.

If you like your Martini on the rocks, fill your glass halfway up with cracked ice and pour in the chilled Martini. A word of caution: don't crack the ice too finely or it will melt too fast. Cubes cracked to about half size are perfect.

Can you get a running head start on icing the Martini by mixing it ahead of time and storing it in the refrigerator? Although this is done now and then, the result can never be that Perfect Martini. The moment the vermouth combines with the gin or vodka, an immediate but short-lived chemical reaction occurs. Bernard de Voto put it well: "You can no more keep a Martini in the refrigerator than you can keep a kiss there."

If you want a bit more of a head start, however, store both your gin and vermouth there. That way you'll always be starting off with cold ingredients.

Now you are ready. The ingredients have been selected with care. The gin. The vodka. The vermouth. The garnish. The tools are all at hand. And the glassware sparkles. All is in preparation, ready to mix a fine Dry Martini . . . the Perfect Martini.

Casino Cocktail
2 oz. Old Tom gin
2 dashes orange bitters
¼ oz. Maraschino
   liqueur
¼ oz. lemon juice

THE MARTINI HOUR

ROM THAT moment in the mid-1800s when sweet gin was first blended with sweet vermouth, the Martini has been a very special drink.

It was the Martini that helped turn America away from straight whiskey and on to mixed drinks. It was the Martini that many women first enjoyed when social drinking was liberated from a "for men only" to "mixed company" activity. And it was the Martini that spawned a cult fanaticism that looks upon the "Martini Hour" as a sacred rite.

It is also the Martini that frequently generates headlines from Washington, D.C.

John Kennedy, while still a senator, singled out the Martini as a symbol of special privilege at taxpayers' expense when he created the phrase "Martini lunch" to describe business dining.

George McGovern, when campaigning for president, continued the attack on tax-deductible entertaining, but he upped the

Chatterly
2 oz. dry gin
½ oz. dry vermouth
¼ oz. orange curaçao

89

ante when he lashed out first against the "three-Martini lunch," then toned that down to attacks on a more credible "two-Martini lunch."

Jimmy Carter was not so restrained, however, and made headlines proposing tax reform that would end taxpayer-supported "three-Martini lunches." (Natural progression would indicate that the next Democratic candidate will attack the "four-Martini lunch.")

The Martini, however, has not always been held in disrepute by the White House. Franklin Roosevelt cherished his four-part-gin, one-part-vermouth Martinis, enjoying two — no more, no less — before dinner each night. Richard Nixon was known to favor Martinis and, for one of his rare flirtations with the White House press corps, invited them upstairs one snowy New Year's Eve and personally mixed Martinis and led a toast to the New Year, 1971. Gerald Ford was another Martini enthusiast, frequently relaxing with two five-to-one Martinis before dining.

To presidents and commoners, workingmen and practitioners of leisure, the Martini and cocktail hour are the perfect marriage. The chilled crystal alive with beads of frost. The union of clear, crisp gin and golden-hued vermouth. The streak of yellow lemon peel,

Jean Harlow, deciding which drink to down, in The Girl from Missouri.

gently twisted and subtle with flavor. Or the well-rounded olive studded with a flash of flaming red pimiento. The King of Cocktails, the Dry Martini. Little wonder it is the perfect cocktail for that glorious time of day, the cocktail hour, the Martini Hour. A time to relax and reflect. A time when all the pieces take their rightful place . . . and the day comes into focus. A time when those nagging, gnawing problems don't seem quite that serious after all. A time, in fact, when humor emerges from tribulation . . . and the crisis of the day becomes a subject for laughter. The Martini Hour: when friendships are rekindled and relationships reborn.

Chicago Martini
2 oz. dry gin
½ oz. Scotch
Green olive

2 6 8 PERFECT MARTINIS

O THE PURIST, a Martini is a simple thing. Dry gin. A little vermouth. An olive, or perhaps a twist of lemon peel. And that's it. Nothing more. Proportions change; not the ingredients.

Yet, while many drink Martinis — and nothing but Martinis — they have yet to be totally satisfied. So they constantly look for a Martini that's a little different. A better Martini. A Perfect Martini.

This search for perfection has led to the creation of hundreds of different kinds of Martinis. Not only have the proportions of basic ingredients changed, but there are substitutions in the ingredients themselves. Basically, all are a blending of a clear, distilled spirit and a fortified, flavored wine. But sometimes a liqueur is added. Or brandy. Or fruit juice. Or even egg white. Most anything can, and often does, turn up in these ingenious variations.

And the names that identify these drinks

Classic Dry Martini
2 parts London dry gin
1 part French vermouth
1 dash orange bitters

can be as inventive as the recipes. Many are
simply named for a person — sometimes their
creator, sometimes a personality, sometimes a
friend: Jack Sloat, Jimmy Blanc, Gene
Tunney, Eddie Brown, Queen Elizabeth,
Peggy, Barry, Walter, Diana, Dr. Monahan.
Others are named for places: Greenbrier,
Hotel Plaza, Lamb's Club, Hoffman House.
And others are descriptive names: Gloom
Chaser, Liar's Cocktail, Depth Charge, Hanky
Panky, Tonight or Never, One Exciting Night
(just try ordering that at the corner bar).
They range from an Addison to a Zaza . . .
and each is different.

But not one of them has become everyone's
favorite Martini. So here are the remaining
recipes for two hundred and sixty-eight personal favorites — each a Perfect Martini to
someone, somewhere.

94

Club Cocktail

1½ oz. dry gin
¾ oz. sweet vermouth
¼ oz. yellow
  Chartreuse
Cherry or green olive

Cooperstown

4 parts dry gin
1 part French
  vermouth
1 part Italian vermouth
1 dash orange bitters
1 dash Angostura
  bitters
Sprig of mint bruised
  and stirred with each
  cocktail
Twist of lemon peel

Copenhagen

1 oz. dry gin
1 oz. Aquavit
½ oz. dry vermouth
Green olive

Coronet

2 oz. dry gin
¾ oz. port wine
Twist of lemon peel

Crocker

1½ oz. dry gin
½ oz. sweet vermouth
½ oz. dry vermouth

Deep Sea

1½ oz. Old Tom gin
1 oz. dry vermouth
1 dash orange bitters
¼ oz. Pernod
Twist of lemon peel

Delmonico

1 oz. dry gin
½ oz. dry vermouth
½ oz. sweet vermouth
½ oz. Cognac
1 dash Angostura
  bitters
Orange peel

Depth Charge

1¼ oz. dry gin
1¼ oz. Lillet
¼ oz. Pernod
Orange peel

Dernier Round

1½ oz. dry gin
½ oz. dry vermouth
¼ oz. Cognac
¼ oz. Cointreau
1 dash Angostura
  bitters

Dewey

1¼ oz. dry gin
1¼ oz. dry vermouth
1 dash orange bitters

Diana

1½ oz. dry gin
¾ oz. dry vermouth
¼ oz. sweet vermouth
¼ oz. Pernod
Twist of lemon peel

Dillatine

Mix a Dry Martini to
your favorite propor-
tions, but add a dilly
bean instead of the
green olive or twist of
lemon peel.

Dixie

2 oz. dry gin
¼ oz. dry vermouth
¼ oz. Pernod

Dr. Monahan

2 oz. dry gin
¼ oz. Pernod
1 dash orange bitters
Twist of lemon peel

Douglas

1¾ oz. dry gin
¾ oz. dry vermouth
Orange peel or twist of
lemon peel

Dry Martini

2 oz. dry gin
½ oz. dry vermouth
Green olive or twist of
lemon peel

Du Barry Cocktail

1½ oz. dry gin
¾ oz. dry vermouth
¼ oz. Pernod
1 dash Angostura
 bitters
Orange slice

Eddie Brown

1¾ oz. dry gin
¾ oz. Lillet
2 dashes apricot
 brandy
Twist of lemon peel

Elegant

1¾ oz. dry gin
½ oz. dry vermouth
¼ oz. Grand Marnier

Elephant's Ear

1 oz. dry gin
¾ oz. dry vermouth
¾ oz. Dubonnet

El Presidente

1¾ oz. light rum
¾ oz. dry vermouth
1 dash Angostura
 bitters

Enos

1¾ oz. dry gin
¾ oz. dry vermouth
¼ oz. Pernod
Cherry

Escobar Martini

7 parts tequila
1 part dry vermouth
Green olive

Fare-Thee-Well

1½ oz. dry gin
½ oz. dry vermouth
¼ oz. sweet vermouth
¼ oz. orange curaçao

Farmer's Cocktail

1½ oz. dry gin
½ oz. sweet vermo: th
½ oz. dry vermouth
2 dashes Angostura
 bitters

Fascinator

1¾ oz. dry gin
½ oz. dry vermouth
¼ oz. Pernod
Sprig of mint

Fernet Branca
Cocktail

1½ oz. dry gin
½ oz. sweet vermouth
½ oz. Fernet Branca
Cherry

Fifth Avenue

1½ oz. dry gin
½ oz. dry vermouth
½ oz. Fernet Branca

Fifty Fifty

1¼ oz. dry gin
1¼ oz. dry vermouth
Green olive

Fin de Siècle
Cocktail

1½ oz. dry gin
¾ oz. sweet vermouth
¼ oz. Amer Picon
1 dash orange bitters

Fino Martini

2 oz. dry gin
½ oz. fino sherry
Green olive or twist of
lemon peel

Flying Dutchman

7 parts dry gin
1 part French
  vermouth
2 dashes orange
  curaçao

Foggy Day

1½ oz. dry gin
¼ oz. Pernod
Twist of lemon peel

Shake and pour over
ice.

Fourth Degree

¾ oz. dry gin
¾ oz. dry vermouth
¾ oz. sweet vermouth
¼ oz. Pernod
Twist of lemon peel

Gene Tunney

1¾ oz. dry gin
¾ oz. dry vermouth
1 dash lemon juice
1 dash orange juice
Cherry

Gibson

7 parts dry gin
1 part French
  vermouth
Cocktail onion

Gibson Girl

1¼ oz. Old Tom gin
1¼ oz. dry vermouth
Twist of lemon peel

Gin

2 oz. dry gin
2 dashes orange bitters
Twist of lemon or
orange peel

Gin and French

Coat the inside of a
glass with dry ver-
mouth. Fill the glass
with 2¼ oz. dry gin.

Ginka

1¼ oz. dry gin
1¼ oz. vodka
½ oz. dry vermouth
Twist of lemon peel or
green olive

Gin 'n' It

3 parts dry gin
1 part Italian vermouth
Twist of lemon peel

Put large ice cubes in
an Old-Fashioned
glass. Pour gin three-
quarters of the way up
the glass. Pour ver-
mouth over the gin to
fill the glass. Twist a
strip of lemon peel
over the drink, splash-
ing oil on the surface.
Drop the peel into the
glass. Serve with a
swizzle stick.

Gloom Chaser

5 parts dry gin
1 part French
  vermouth
2 dashes Pernod
2 dashes grenadine

Golden Ermine

1½ oz. dry gin
¾ oz. dry vermouth
¼ oz. sweet vermouth

Golden Girl

1¾ oz. dry gin
¾ oz. dry sherry
1 dash orange bitters
1 dash Angostura
  bitters

Golden Martini

7 parts golden-colored
  dry gin
1 part French
  vermouth
Twist of lemon peel

Golf

1¾ oz. dry gin
¾ oz. dry vermouth
2 dashes Angostura
  bitters

Gordon

5 parts dry gin
1 part amontillado
  sherry
Cocktail onion

Great Secret

1¾ oz. dry gin
¾ oz. Lillet
1 dash Angostura
  bitters
Orange peel

Greenbrier

2 parts dry gin
1 part Italian vermouth
Sprig of mint bruised
  and stirred with each
  cocktail
Twist of lemon peel

Guards

1¾ oz. dry gin
¾ oz. sweet vermouth
¼ oz. orange curacao
Orange peel or cherry

Gunga Din

3 parts dry gin
1 part dry vermouth
Juice of ¼ orange

Shake. Garnish with a
pineapple slice.

Gypsy

1¼ oz. dry gin
1¼ oz. sweet vermouth
Cherry

Hakam

1¼ oz. dry gin
1¼ oz. sweet vermouth
¼ oz. orange curaçao
1 dash orange bitters
Cherry

Half and Half

3 parts dry gin
3 parts vodka
1 part French
  vermouth
Twist of lemon peel

H and H

1¾ oz. dry gin
¾ oz. Lillet
¼ oz. orange curacao
Orange peel

Hanky Panky

1¾ oz. dry gin
¾ oz. sweet vermouth
¼ oz. Fernet Branca
Orange peel

Harold's Martini

(for those who never
have more than one!)

4 oz. dry gin
½ oz. French
  vermouth
1 dash orange bitters

Stir and pour into a
6-oz. carafe. Bury the
carafe in shaved ice
and serve with a frosted
cocktail glass and a
stuffed green olive.

Harry's

1¾ oz. dry gin
¾ oz. sweet vermouth
¼ oz. Pernod
2 sprigs of mint
Mint leaf

Hasty Cocktail

1¼ oz. dry gin
¾ oz. dry vermouth
¼ oz. grenadine
1 dash Pernod

Hearst

1¼ oz. dry gin
1¼ oz. sweet vermouth
1 dash orange bitters
1 dash Angostura
  bitters

Hilliard

1¼ oz. dry gin
¾ oz. sweet vermouth
1 dash Peychaud's
  bitters

Hillsboro

1¾ oz. dry gin
¾ oz. dry vermouth
1 dash orange bitters
1 dash Angostura
  bitters

Hoffman House

1¾ oz. dry gin
¾ oz. French
  vermouth
2 dashes orange bitters
Green olive

Homestead

1¾ oz. dry gin
¾ oz. sweet vermouth
Orange slice

Muddle fruit in glass
or mixer.

Hong Kong

2 parts dry gin
1 part French
   vermouth
¼ tsp. sugar syrup
1 tsp. lime juice
1 dash Angostura
   bitters

Honolulu
Hurricane

4 parts dry gin
1 part French
   vermouth
1 part Italian vermouth
1 tsp. pineapple juice

Shake.

Hotel Plaza

1 oz. dry gin
¾ oz. French
   vermouth
¾ oz. Italian vermouth

Fill a glass with ice.
Garnish with a pine-
apple spear.

H.P.W.

2 oz. dry gin
¼ oz. French
   vermouth
¼ oz. Italian vermouth
Orange peel

Imperial

1¼ oz. dry gin
1¼ oz. dry vermouth
1 dash Angostura
   bitters
¼ tsp. Maraschino
   liqueur
Cherry or green olive

Inca

¾ oz. dry gin
¾ oz. dry sherry
½ oz. French
   vermouth
½ oz. Italian vermouth
1 dash Orgeat syrup
1 dash orange bitters

Indispensable

1½ oz. dry gin
½ oz. French
   vermouth
½ oz. Italian vermouth
¼ oz. Pernod

International

4 parts dry gin
1 part French
   vermouth
1 part Italian vermouth
2 dashes crème de
   cassis

Jack Sloat

1½ oz. dry gin
½ oz. sweet vermouth
¼ oz. dry vermouth
2 slices pineapple

Shake.

Jackson

1¼ oz. dry gin
1¼ oz. Dubonnet
2 dashes orange bitters

James Bond

3 parts Gordon's dry
   gin
1 part vodka
½ part Kina Lillet

Shake. Add a large,
thin slice of lemon.

Jeyplak

1½ oz. dry gin
¾ oz. sweet vermouth
¼ oz. Pernod
Twist of lemon peel

Jimmy Blanc

1¾ oz. dry gin
¾ oz. Lillet
¼ oz. Dubonnet
Orange peel

J.O.S.

¾ oz. dry gin
¾ oz. dry vermouth
¾ oz. sweet vermouth
1 dash brandy
1 dash orange bitters
1 dash lemon juice
Twist of lemon peel

Journalist

1½ oz. dry gin
¼ oz. sweet vermouth
¼ oz. dry vermouth
1 dash Angostura
  bitters
1 dash lemon juice
1 dash orange curaçao

Jungle

1 oz. dry gin
¾ oz. sweet vermouth
¾ oz. sherry

Juniper

2 oz. dry gin
½ oz. dry vermouth
1 dash grenadine

Kahlúa Martini

2 oz. dry gin
½ oz. Kahlúa
Twist of lemon peel

Kangaroo

1¾ oz. vodka
¾ oz. dry vermouth
Twist of lemon peel

Kina

1½ oz. dry gin
½ oz. sweet vermouth
½ oz. Kina Lillet
Cherry

Knickerbocker

1½ oz. dry gin
¾ oz. dry vermouth
¼ oz. sweet vermouth
Twist of lemon peel

Kup's Indispensable

1½ oz. dry gin
½ oz. Italian vermouth
½ oz. French
  vermouth
1 dash bitters
Orange peel

Ladies' Choice

1¼ oz. dry gin
½ oz. dry vermouth
¼ oz. kümmel

Lamb's Club

4 parts dry gin
1 part French
  vermouth
1 part Italian vermouth
2 dashes Benedictine
Twist of lemon peel

Last Round

1 oz. dry gin
1 oz. dry vermouth
¼ oz. brandy
¼ oz. Pernod

Leap Year

1¼ oz. dry gin
½ oz. orange-
   flavored gin
½ oz. sweet vermouth
¼ oz. lemon juice

Liar's Cocktail

1½ oz. dry gin
½ oz. dry vermouth
¼ oz. orange curaçao
¼ oz. sweet vermouth

Licia Albanese

1½ oz. dry gin
½ oz. Campari
Twist of lemon peel

Serve over ice.

Lillet Cocktail

1½ oz. Lillet
1 oz. dry gin
Twist of lemon peel

Lone Tree

2 parts dry gin
1 part Italian vermouth
1 dash lemon juice

Louis

1½ oz. dry gin
½ oz. dry vermouth
¼ oz. Grand Marnier
¼ oz. Cointreau

Lucien Gaudin

1 oz. dry gin
½ oz. Cointreau
½ oz. Campari
½ oz. dry vermouth

Mandarin

1 oz. dry gin
1 oz. dry vermouth
¼ oz. orange curaçao
¼ oz. Mandarinette

Marguerite

2 parts dry gin
1 part dry vermouth
1 dash Angostura
   bitters
Twist of orange peel
Maraschino cherry

Martinez

1¼ oz. dry gin
1¼ oz. sweet
   vermouth
1 dash bitters
1 dash sugar syrup

Martini

1¾ oz. dry gin
¾ oz. dry vermouth
Green olive

Martini
Holland-Style

2 oz. Dutch gin
½ oz. dry vermouth
Twist of lemon peel

Martini Special

(serves six)
8 jiggers dry gin
3 jiggers Italian
   vermouth
⅔ jigger Orange
   Flower Water
1 dash Angostura
   bitters

Stir and serve with
maraschino cherries.

Maurice

2 parts dry gin
1 part French
  vermouth
1 part Italian vermouth
Juice of ¼ orange
1 dash Angostura
  bitters

Maxim

2 parts dry gin
1 part Italian vermouth
2 dashes white
  crème de cacao

Mecca

¾ oz. dry gin
¾ oz. dry vermouth
½ oz. sweet vermouth
½ oz. orange juice

Shake.

Medium Martini

4 parts dry gin
1 part French
  vermouth
1 part Italian vermouth
1 dash orange bitters
1 dash Angostura
  bitters

Merry-Go-Round

1½ oz. dry gin
½ oz. sweet vermouth
½ oz. dry vermouth
Green olive
Twist of lemon peel

Merry Widower

1 part dry gin
1 part dry vermouth
2 dashes Benedictine
1 dash Peychaud's
  bitters
2 dashes Pernod
Twist of lemon peel

Mickey Finn

1 oz. dry gin
1 oz. dry vermouth
¼ oz. Pernod
¼ oz. white crème de
  menthe
Sprig of mint

Midnight

¾ oz. dry gin
¾ oz. sweet vermouth
¾ oz. dry vermouth
¼ oz. Pernod
1 dash orange juice

Minnehaha

1 oz. dry gin
½ oz. dry vermouth
½ oz. sweet vermouth
½ oz. orange juice

Float a teaspoonful of
Pernod on the surface.

Modder Cocktail

1½ oz. dry gin
½ oz. dry vermouth
½ oz. Dubonnet
Twist of lemon peel

Montpelier

1¼ oz. dry gin
¾ oz. dry vermouth
Cocktail onion

Moonshine

1¾ oz. dry gin
½ oz. dry vermouth
¼ oz. Maraschino
    liqueur
2 dashes Pernod

Naked Martini

3 oz. dry gin
Twist of lemon peel or
green olive

Naval Cocktail

1¼ oz. dry gin
1¼ oz. sweet
    vermouth
Cocktail onion
Twist of lemon peel

Negroni

1 oz. dry gin
1 oz. sweet vermouth
1 oz. Campari

Newberry

1 oz. dry gin
1 oz. sweet vermouth
½ oz. orange curaçao
Twist of lemon or
orange peel

New Yorker

1½ oz. dry vermouth
½ oz. dry gin
½ oz. dry sherry
1 dash Cointreau

Nineteen Twenty

1½ oz. dry gin
½ oz. dry vermouth
½ oz. Kirschwasser
1 dash orange bitters
1 dash Groseille syrup

Number 3

1¾ oz. dry gin
½ oz. dry vermouth
1 dash orange bitters
¼ oz. anisette

Number 6

1¾ oz. dry gin
½ oz. sweet vermouth
¼ oz. orange curacao
Twist of lemon peel
Orange peel
Cherry

Old Etonian

1¼ oz. dry gin
1¼ oz. Lillet
2 dashes orange bitters
2 dashes crème de
    noyaux
Orange peel

Olympic

1¾ oz. dry gin
½ oz. sweet vermouth
¼ oz. Pernod

One Exciting
Night

¾ oz. dry gin
¾ oz. dry vermouth
¾ oz. sweet vermouth
¼ oz. orange juice
Twist of lemon peel

Coat the rim of the
glass with sugar before
mixing.

Nome

7 parts dry gin
1 part dry sherry
1 dash Chartreuse

One of Mine

1 oz. dry gin
½ oz. sweet vermouth
½ oz. dry vermouth
½ oz. orange juice
1 dash bitters

Original Martini (Martinez)

1 wineglass sweet
  vermouth
1 pony Old Tom gin
2 dashes bitters
1 dash Maraschino
  liqueur

Shake with two small
lumps of ice. Add a
quarter slice of lemon
and serve.

Pacific-Union Club Martini

5 parts Old Tom gin
1 part dry vermouth
Twist of lemon peel or
green olive

Paisley Martini

2¼ oz. dry gin
¼ oz. dry vermouth
1 dash Scotch

Pall Mall

¾ oz. dry gin
¾ oz. dry vermouth
¾ oz. sweet vermouth
¼ oz. white crème de
  menthe
1 dash orange bitters

Parisian

5 parts dry gin
1 part French
  vermouth
3 dashes crème de
  cassis
Twist of lemon peel

Peggy

1½ oz. dry gin
¾ oz. dry vermouth
¼ oz. Pernod
¼ oz. Dubonnet

Perfect

2 oz. dry gin
¼ oz. French
  vermouth
¼ oz. Italian
  vermouth
1 dash bitters
Twist of lemon peel

Perfection

1¾ oz. dry gin
½ oz. sweet vermouth
½ oz. orange juice

Perfect Royal

¾ oz. dry gin
¾ oz. dry vermouth
¾ oz. sweet vermouth
¼ oz. Pernod
Green cherry

Pernod Martini

2 oz. dry gin
½ oz. dry vermouth
1 dash Pernod

Piccadilly

1½ oz. dry gin
¾ oz. dry vermouth
¼ oz. Pernod
1 dash grenadine

Pink Gin

Fill an Old-Fashioned
glass with cracked ice.
Add 2 dashes bitters
and 2½ oz. dry gin.

Plaza

¾ oz. dry gin
¾ oz. dry vermouth
¾ oz. sweet vermouth

Shake with ice. Add a
slice of pineapple.

Plymouth
Cocktail

2½ oz. dry gin
2 dashes orange bitters

Poet's Dream

1 oz. dry gin
¾ oz. dry vermouth
¾ oz. Benedictine
Twist of lemon peel

Polo

1 oz. dry gin
½ oz. dry vermouth
½ oz. sweet vermouth
½ oz. lime juice

Pom Pom

1½ oz. dry vermouth
¾ oz. dry gin
2 dashes orange bitters

Princeton

1½ oz. dry gin
1 oz. port
2 dashes orange bitters
Twist of lemon peel

Psychedelic
Martini

6 parts dry gin
1 part French
    vermouth
1 part Italian vermouth
½ part orange juice
½ part pineapple juice
1 dash anisette

Shake.

Punt é Mes
Negroni

¾ oz. dry gin
¾ oz. sweet vermouth
¾ oz. Punt é Mes
Twist of lemon peel

Puritan

1¾ oz. dry gin
½ oz. dry vermouth
¼ oz. yellow
    Chartreuse
1 dash orange bitters

Queen Elizabeth

1¾ oz. dry gin
½ oz. dry vermouth
¼ oz. Benedictine

Queen Martini

2 parts dry gin
1 part Italian vermouth
1 part French
    vermouth
1 dash orange bitters
1 dash Angostura
    bitters

Racquet Club

1¾ oz. dry gin
¾ oz. dry vermouth
1 dash orange bitters
Orange peel

Raidme

1¾ oz. dry gin
½ oz. Pernod
¼ oz. Campari

Ramon

1½ oz. dry gin
½ oz. dry vermouth
½ oz. Hercules

Rattler

¾ oz. dry gin
¾ oz. French
    vermouth
¾ oz. Italian
    vermouth
½ oz. orange juice

RCA Special

1½ oz. dry gin
½ oz. dry vermouth
½ oz. sweet vermouth
2 dashes orange bitters
Orange peel

Rendezvous

1½ oz. dry gin
½ oz. Kirschwasser
¼ oz. Campari
Twist of lemon peel

Rex

1¾ oz. dry gin
¾ oz. sweet vermouth
1 dash orange bitters

Richmond

1¾ oz. dry gin
¾ oz. Lillet
Twist of lemon peel

Roller Derby

1¾ oz. dry gin
¼ oz. dry vermouth
¼ oz. sweet vermouth
¼ oz. Benedictine

Rolls Roya

1¼ oz. dry gin
½ oz. sweet vermouth
½ oz. dry vermouth
¼ oz. Benedictine

Rolls-Royce

1½ oz. dry gin
½ oz. dry vermouth
½ oz. sweet vermouth
2 dashes Benedictine

Roma

1½ oz. dry gin
½ oz. sweet vermouth
½ oz. dry vermouth
3 fresh strawberries,
    mixed with drink

Rosa

1½ oz. dry gin
½ oz. dry vermouth
½ oz. cherry-flavored
    brandy

Rose du Boy

1½ oz. dry gin
½ oz. dry vermouth
¼ oz. cherry-flavored
    brandy
¼ oz. Kirschwasser

Roselyn

1¾ oz. dry gin
½ oz. dry vermouth
¼ oz. grenadine
Twist of lemon peel

Rose Marie

1¼ oz. dry gin
½ oz. dry vermouth
¼ oz. Armagnac
¼ oz. cherry-flavored
  brandy
¼ oz. Campari

Rosington

1¾ oz. dry gin
¾ oz. sweet vermouth
Orange peel

Royal Cocktail

1¾ oz. dry gin
¾ oz. Dubonnet
1 dash orange bitters
1 dash Angostura
  bitters

Rum Martini

5 parts light rum
1 part French
  vermouth
Twist of lemon peel

Saketini

2 oz. dry gin
½ oz. sake
Twist of lemon peel

Salome

1 oz. dry gin
¾ oz. dry vermouth
¾ oz. Dubonnet

San Martin

¾ oz. dry gin
¾ oz. dry vermouth
¾ oz. sweet vermouth
¼ oz. anisette
1 dash bitters

Satan's Whiskers

½ oz. dry gin
½ oz. dry vermouth
½ oz. sweet vermouth
½ oz. orange juice
¼ oz. Grand Marnier
¼ oz. orange bitters

Savoy

1¾ oz. dry gin
½ oz. dry vermouth
¼ oz. Dubonnet
Orange peel

Savoy Hotel Special

1½ oz. dry gin
½ oz. dry vermouth
1 dash Pernod
2 dashes grenadine
Twist of lemon peel

Schnozzle

¾ oz. dry gin
¾ oz. dry vermouth
½ oz. cocktail sherry
¼ oz. Pernod
¼ oz. orange curaçao

Self-Starter

1½ oz. dry gin
¾ oz. Lillet
¼ oz. apricot-flavored
  brandy
2 dashes Pernod

Seventh Regiment

1¾ oz. dry gin
¾ oz. sweet vermouth
2 twists of lemon peel

Stir twists with drink.

Sherry Cocktail

2 oz. dry sherry
½ oz. dry vermouth
2 dashes orange bitters

Silver Bullet

2 oz. dry gin
¼ oz. dry vermouth

Stir. Float ¼ oz.
Scotch on the surface.

Silver Cocktail

1 oz. dry gin
1 oz. dry vermouth
2 dashes orange bitters
¼ tsp. sugar
¼ oz. Maraschino
  liqueur
Twist of lemon peel

Smiler

1¼ oz. dry gin
½ oz. dry vermouth
½ oz. sweet vermouth
¼ oz. orange juice
1 dash Angostura
  bitters

Shake.

Smoky Martini

7 parts dry gin
1 part Scotch
Twist of lemon peel

Snyder

1¾ oz. dry gin
½ oz. dry vermouth
¼ oz. orange curaçao
Orange peel

Society

1¾ oz. dry gin
½ oz. dry vermouth
¼ oz. grenadine

Some Mother

1¾ oz. dry gin
½ oz. dry vermouth
¼ oz. Pernod
Cocktail onion

So So

¾ oz. dry gin
¾ oz. sweet vermouth
½ oz. apple brandy
½ oz. grenadine

Sour Kisses

1¾ oz. dry gin
¾ oz. dry vermouth
1 egg white

Shake.

Southern Gin Cocktail

2¼ oz. dry gin
¼ oz. orange curaçao
2 dashes orange bitters

Soviet Salute

1 oz. vodka
¾ oz. dry vermouth
¾ oz. dry sherry

Sphinx

2 oz. dry gin
¼ oz. sweet vermouth
¼ oz. dry vermouth
Lemon wedge

Starlight

1¾ oz. dry gin
¾ oz. orange curacao
1 dash Angostura
  bitters

Shake.

Straight Law

1¾ oz. dry sherry
¾ oz. dry gin
Twist of lemon peel

Strawberry Blonde

7 parts dry gin
1 part Chambraise
  strawberry aperitif
Twist of lemon peel

Submarine

1½ oz. dry gin
½ oz. Dubonnet
½ oz. dry vermouth
1 dash Boker's bitters

Sunshine

1¾ oz. dry gin
¾ oz. sweet vermouth
1 dash bitters
Twist of orange peel

Sweet Martini

2 parts dry gin
1 part Italian vermouth
1 dash orange bitters
1 dash Angostura
  bitters

Tammany

¾ oz. dry gin
¾ oz. dry vermouth
¾ oz. sweet vermouth
¼ oz. Pernod

Tequini

2 oz. tequila
½ oz. dry vermouth
Green olive or twist of
lemon peel

Third Degree

1½ oz. dry gin
¾ oz. dry vermouth
¼ oz. Pernod

Tío Pepe Martini

7 parts dry gin
1 part Tío Pepe sherry
Twist of lemon peel

Tonight or Never

1 oz. dry gin
1 oz. dry vermouth
½ oz. Cognac

Trilby

1¼ oz. dry gin
1 oz. sweet vermouth
2 dashes orange bitters

Stir. Float ¼ oz. crème
d'Yvette on the surface.

Trinity

1 oz. dry gin
¾ oz. dry vermouth
¾ oz. sweet vermouth

Trio

¾ oz. dry gin
¾ oz. dry vermouth
¾ oz. sweet vermouth

Turf

1 oz. dry gin
1 oz. dry vermouth
¼ oz. Pernod
2 dashes Angostura
  bitters
Orange peel

Tuxedo

1¼ oz. dry gin
1¼ oz. dry vermouth
¼ oz. Maraschino
  liqueur
¼ tsp. Pernod
2 dashes orange bitters
Twist of lemon peel

Union League

1¾ oz. Old Tom gin
¾ oz. port wine
1 dash orange bitters

Upissippi

1½ oz. dry gin
½ oz. sweet vermouth
½ oz. dry vermouth
¼ oz. grenadine

Vampire

1 oz. dry gin
1 oz. dry vermouth
½ oz. lime juice

Shake.

Van

1¾ oz. dry gin
½ oz. dry vermouth
¼ oz. Grand Marnier

Vancouver

1½ oz. dry gin
¾ oz. sweet vermouth
¼ oz. Benedictine
1 dash orange bitters

Shake.

Velocity

1½ oz. sweet vermouth
¾ oz. dry gin
Orange slice

Shake.

Vendôme

1 oz. dry gin
1 oz. Dubonnet
½ oz. dry vermouth
Twist of lemon peel

Vermouth Rinse

Coat the inside of a
glass with dry ver-
mouth. Shake off the
excess. Fill the glass
with chilled dry gin.
Add a twist of lemon
peel or a green olive.

Vermouth Triple Sec

1 oz. dry vermouth
1 oz. dry gin
½ oz. Triple Sec
2 dashes orange bitters
Twist of lemon peel

Very Dry Martini

5 parts dry gin
1 part French
  vermouth
Twist of lemon peel

Victor

1½ oz. dry vermouth
½ oz. dry gin
½ oz. brandy

VIP Martini

Fill a stemmed cock-
tail glass with chilled
dry gin. Waft a fine
spray of dry vermouth
gently on the surface
from an atomizer. Add
a twist of lemon peel
or a green olive.

Vodka Gibson

2 oz. vodka
½ oz. dry vermouth
Cocktail onion

Vodka Martini

2 oz. vodka
½ oz. dry vermouth
Twist of lemon peel or
green olive

Wallick

1¼ oz. dry gin
1¼ oz. dry vermouth
¼ oz. orange curaçao

Walter

5 parts dry gin
½ part dry vermouth
½ part dry sherry
2 drops lemon juice

Warden

1½ oz. dry gin
½ oz. dry vermouth
½ oz. Pernod

Wembley

1½ oz. dry gin
¾ oz. dry vermouth
¼ oz. apple brandy
1 dash apricot-flavored
  brandy

White Pelican

1¾ oz. dry gin
½ oz. dry vermouth
¼ oz. sweet vermouth

Wild Rose

1½ oz. dry gin
½ oz. dry vermouth
½ oz. sweet vermouth
1 dash orange bitters
1 dash Angostura
  bitters

Wilson Special

2 oz. dry gin
¼ oz. dry vermouth
2 orange slices

Shake.

Yachting Club

1¾ oz. Hollands gin
¾ oz. dry vermouth
2 dashes Peychaud's
  bitters
1 dash Pernod

Sweeten with sugar to
taste.

Yale

1¾ oz. dry gin
½ oz. dry vermouth
2 dashes orange bitters
¼ oz. Maraschino
   liqueur

Sweeten with sugar to
taste.

Yellow Daisy

1½ oz. dry gin
½ oz. dry vermouth
¼ oz. Grand Marnier
¼ oz. Pernod
Cherry

Yolanda

¾ oz. dry gin
¾ oz. brandy
½ oz. sweet vermouth
¼ oz. grenadine
¼ oz. Pernod

York

7 parts dry gin
1 part French
   vermouth
1 drop of Scotch
Twist of lemon peel

Zaza

1¾ oz. Old Tom gin
¾ oz. Dubonnet
1 dash orange bitters

CREDITS

115

ABOUT THE AUTHOR

Robert Herzbrun is a vice-president of one of Southern California's leading advertising agencies and a regular contributor to *Los Angeles* magazine, and he has written several books on food and restaurants. He lives in Sherman Oaks, California, with his wife and three children.